otherwise elsewhere

Books by David Rivard

Torque
Wise Poison
Bewitched Playground
Sugartown
Otherwise Elsewhere

otherwise elsewhere

poems

david rivard

graywolf press

This publication is made possible by funding provided in part by a grant from the Minnesota State Arts Board, through an appropriation by the Minnesota State Legislature, a grant from the National Endowment for the Arts, and private funders. Significant support has also been provided by Target; the McKnight Foundation; and other generous contributions from foundations, corporations, and individuals. To these organizations and individuals we offer our heartfelt thanks.

Published by Graywolf Press
250 Third Avenue North, Suite 600
Minneapolis, Minnesota 55401

www.graywolfpress.org

Published in the United States of America

ISBN 978-1-55597-573-9

2   4   6   8   9   7   5   3   1
First Graywolf Printing, 2011

Library of Congress Control Number: 2010937511

Cover design: Michaela Sullivan

Cover art: *The Cosmos*, 1750. From "An Original Theory or New Hypothesis of the Universe" by Thomas Wright. British Library, London, Great Britain. Photo credit: HIP / Art Resource, New York.

for Simone

here everywhere

Contents

otherwise elsewhere

Otherwise Elsewhere

Otherwise elsewhere—someone somewhere other than here—
the stable-hand for an equestrian team or the bodhisattva
stretched out by the river or the sleepwalking knife-thrower,
the dubious bridegroom or the dental hygienist or steamfitter—
otherwise, the contented singer of karaoke—otherwise that
whoreson of the adamantine, an anti-semite with a pyramid scheme,
the small town doctor with TB—elsewise, in a soaking tub,
a tenured gnostic or a tan Micawber; elsewise Joey "Crazy Joe" Gallo
in Umberto's clam bar; or in Berlin, at the Atelier Jacobi,
Lotte Jacobi; elsewise the Secretary of Defense, a conductor
of souls, or a swimmer resuscitated by a wolfhound, or a policeman
eating beer-battered shrimp, or what used to be called an industrialist—
otherwise, a nun about to go over the wall—elsewise, at auction dock,
either one of the deckhands off-loading bushel-baskets of littlenecks
or the Irish wholesaler with his whitebait & herring, his glistening
eels on chipped ice & the sawdust wet with blood—otherwise,
the clerk at a lighting outlet—or someone steered by brighter
signs, a settler or a currency trader—elsewise the rooster-brain
who stunned Ophelia—or even Ophelia herself, her boots
made of patent-leather like clement black candles in the rain—
otherwise, aboard the bus from Tetuan to Fez, the Moroccan boy
with his lunch of hardboiled eggs—or a dumbfounded skeptic
or a vixen or a lotus-eater or grandmother or unbaptized doorman—
all those lives & destinations that might have been mine, but weren't—
because there are two kinds of distance between us—towards, & away.

Outbound Fall River 1967

OK then, you know how it is
when you're thirteen, & deep
inside the factory bosses' graveyard?—your hair
damp, atmospherically

violet in the August dusk—the children
you run with calling back
over gravestones & wrought-iron Grand
Army of the Republic

picket fences—in this cemetery
catty-corner
from the *China Inn* (Catholic chow mein
sandwiches

served there Fridays,
Wayne Yee's family cooks them)—
you know all those
grassy family plots you walk over, strongholds

of the cotton mill clans—
Durfees & Taylors, Bordens,
profligate Howlands, & Slades—by way of those
Protestant names afraid & happily

keyed up both, you
know how you suddenly pass through yourself
as the simplest
of questions—like,

you'll have to sign
your name how many times
in this life?
A fixed number you

can never know. Remember
how it feels?—
as if a railway line runs
through the middle of the cemetery,

and for a moment you're riding
in trans-migration to some pure-land oasis, Jerusalem
jetty, or primeval
enhancement, & it might go on & on.

Wordsworthian

The brain bounces forward too, right?
so why return to what yesterday seemed to be becoming
before it became today?—no need for meanness or envy,
no reasons for fear when waking in the morning—
just an unlikely Rose of Sharon blooming by the branch library
and the balanced light of a warming
late October as it shines on a sheet of week-old social studies homework
dropped only recently from the book bag of a wandering Violet Neff
(5 points extra credit—according to Ms. DiNardo, a "nice job"):

nice job say the Tibetans by lugging the rolled-up rugs to air
in front of Yala Carpets mostly the smaller
prayer mats that are colored with clairvoyant vegetable dyes, *nice job*
says the scent of heavenly inventions like the breakfast plantains frying,
well done says the toddler with the jelly-fish haircut,
all answers perfect say the hedgerows of boxwood left
untrimmed by the vestry at St. Augustine's
(a coven of swallows with ADD muttering one-liners within),
perfect say the chicken legs in the freezer case at Fresh Killed Poultry

while you wait for the 91 to the Green Line at Lechmere,
a vaguely Wordsworthian subway stop you think
(because the brain knows it's well within its rights to do so)
a second or two before it occurs to you
to wonder if Ms. DiNardo's grading is strict—

so what if it is? thinks the brain,
I can still imagine her first name is Julie whenever
I'd like.

Lives

Like a bit of shoelace snapped-off
and tied back on by tight knot, frayed
each of us lives attached
to the ridiculousness of suffering
according to the Buddhists
needfully, with plenty of precedent & protégés, & of course
just trying to deal. Am I stronger that I once was?—yes—
but is it enough? On the street, parents
with fidgeting babies, students with bulging
backpacks, a millennium or two of ideas
both bone-headed & marvelous—
could I take-up their burdens, even if I wanted to?
What about the smokers? the malted smell of
pipe tobacco a vast stagecraft recalling Chesapeake Bay
and the Eastern Shore as it goes up in smoke.
Or the cemetery staff?—the funeral director, hearse
drivers & gravediggers? Aware as they are
that a headstone is heavy enough
to pin the head in one spot,
they subdue the morning
atmosphere. Tho even for them
perhaps childhood comes back into view
changed once in awhile. As the summer reading lists
that once seemed to me a bore
now look to be filled with insight & care,
with mutiny & courage to spare.
Never again will you find me hating-on those particular books.
Probably you too wanted
to be a dress designer, a rifleman or geneticist
or photographer. A life of so-called action,
of consequence. Perhaps you ought to have lived
your story as a French-cuff economist
hell-bent on improving the lives of grim coal miners.
The street is wide enough to hold my oldest

most dazzling wishes, but not to let me touch them.
Put them alongside the sound
of Pablo Casals near flawless in playing Bach's cello suite tho
and all experience stretches.

Hidden

The pressure-treated pinewood the picnic table is built from
might as well have marched around at Dunsinane as to be
born again & shipped abroad. "There's nothing," the clerk
at the big-box had said, "nothing as rot-resistant, & nothing
as sturdy for the money." So onward we came only to arrive here
as fiercely soft-spoken as all adults handed white wine & beers
and seated on long benches below the window of a napping
nine-month old. Spring frogs where crickets would hide later
in summer along the stream, Virginia creeper & budded pin oak
where the martens & badgers had navigated through snow—
guided by whatever instrumentation their genetics had brought
into play. A place turned so green by grasses it almost feels
a sin to sit there reading a book with a black cover. The Irish
one of us was speaking of how at fourteen she'd quit all that
church life—the kindly or peevish Sisters of Mercy sweeping
school kids up the wide aisles for Communion, white wimples
and black habits the sad wool of virginal housekeepers
dedicated to the poverty-line—I wouldn't bury my face in it
for anything when I cried, she said. Sometimes she wished
to be back in church now but maybe that was only a daydream
for the sake of her baby girl thinking there had better be more
to life than striving & accumulating property & toys—anyway,
she laughed, every child should have some god other than
her parents to defy. "I see men as trees, walking," the man
who was blind told Christ, half-way to being cured. In all
versions of the story the enormity of his change kept secret
strangely. Hidden. "Go not into the town," Christ says,
"nor tell it to any from the town." The possibility of change
concealed. And as the sun set across the river the cabin
casting its lopsided shadow & trying to become bigger & wider
than the mountain. Arguing its case. After that, the secret life.
The dark forest maneuvering in the middle of the dark forest then.

The Same Bourgeois Magic Wherever
the Mailtrain Sets You Down

It's nice—money—don't tell me
it isn't. To have it, to know that you have it
and can get more—

it's the same for us all—
I'm no
exception—& this is not about

psychosocial
critiques, chaste non-attachment, notions
that money is

a tamed slavery & chase
to touch
an elusive amnesia—you don't

like to shove a hand
in your pants pocket & feel the cash
there?—

well-laundered no doubt—
don't tell me that a billfold in a dark pocket
takes the shape

of a trapdoor, or that
when tendered too freely the face
on every ten dollar bill

Alexander Hamilton
the cabalist & duel-fighter looks sorrier
than the skulls

that were strapped with thongs
of greased leather
to the prows of Viking

longboats.
Money is important.
Don't say people

are troubled by matter
forever really—don't go on about
how

after the first funeral
there seems to be only
unfinishedness

for all those aquaculture
engineers, Panamanian waitresses
and bail bondsmen—

so many mailtrains
never to arrive
because of the foaming action

in a failed immune system—
everyone feels that, everybody
understands

that somewhere
a boy of 14 is out riding his bike, wheeling
around his friends,

shouting, *Hey, know what?*
I got expelled ya' know! I just
got expelled.

Achievement

As much as we wish
we can help ourselves to
coming home
and to a pepper-heavy Bloody Mary
and a back pillow
and long flyways flown by dry-cleaned shirts & dresses
pressed silk synthetics
run-up by *favela* girls born-again
in a factory cave strewn with secondhand sewing machines
so that afterwards maybe
as we arrive again as always inside
the smell of filtered sky & clouds crisscrossed by jet fuel
while the dripping green light resinates
off the edges of a red gum's leaves
perhaps we could even call it the family tree
as we float there above it
looking down through the branches
at the test-prep kids applying their sisterly mascara
in the Saab convertible
committed as we are to achievement
no doubt
and having come home once more
for a little while longer
we will be able to go on helping ourselves then
to the Frenched rack of lamb
or an uninhibited pit bull
encrypted lap top
or pen knife—
an accidental & systemic form of self-inventing life—
and the container ships will go on mutating across sea lanes
carrying cartons
of bath towels hardwoods & pixels,
and at some point each of us will know exactly

how it was
that we came to be among
people who are convinced absolutely
convinced
that they know the score.

Powers

Informally I believe in God's powers,
tho not in his presence; & I can see that this has led
     to various momentary advantages, a certain freedom of choice;
and so, like other citizens given half a chance
I have fallen half in love any number of times
with one sonsy actress or another—please insert here,
if you wish, the lips & décolletage of the ineffable Scarlett Johansson,
her air-conditioned tattoos not unlike
those of a thousand bicycle shop clerks—
     and as such in similarly pleasurable ways
I like to watch a black dog enter a drenched field
and immediately soak it up; & have repeatedly & gladly given money
to men & women because they could play the guitar & sing;
and, on my 11th birthday, asked for & received from my parents
a set of cuff links & plated tie pin;
                         my luck has been in friendship & love;
I like to be carried by people & things, & in fact
once stood on the deck of a white hydrofoil
as it did what a white Greek hydrofoil is supposed to do
with burning diesel fuel & water (it made a summer wave off Naxos).

On the other hand, believing in God's powers but not
in his existence may have had some drawbacks, feelings of being
     stranded say; either gone deep into the brine
of my being my self & solitary
lost inside my mind in the invariable infinity of variant neurons,
     or forced to inhabit a planet
with frequent, inexplicable (or all too explicable) episodes of cruelty—
insert here, at the moment, the wrath of the *janjaweed*
in Hashaba Wasit, or elsewhere sweatshops
approved of by theorists of economic development & efficiency
but staffed 15 hours a day by women who
(like my great-aunt Anna Mello) will probably end up with wrists swollen
to twice their size, necks bent

by bad light & balky sewing machines—
        as in the long view it often seems one
unwavering orbit of infected geese, cold refugees, & insurgents
traveling from here to here.

What I mean to say is that God has abandoned both us & his powers—

he's given them up, & they hurtle around inside us.

At Large

A hammered nail is heard by admiring thunderheads—
and with or without do-rag the carpenter
senses the exchange of a message—between anodized nail
and darkening storm pack a code has been passed.
For those of us who need it instruction is everywhere
—especially east of the Appalachians—advice & warnings
that sometimes take the shape of a barista with her boyfriend,
the both of them wearing Defense Department eyeglasses
and high-fiving beneath as much
encouragement as any billboard for cosmetic dentistry can provide.

        But who could take-in
such signs & not feel the need
to change? Here is a message in loosened thread
from a bumptious mediocre tailor, & there is a signal sent
by a daughter happy to bike the five miles
it takes to fetch the shipwrecked morning newspapers,
but where am I headed? Where will the touch go
after I shake the carpenter's hand? And this is often
what happens whenever you open a door at large & get wet
near trees the rain has so many different tasks for.

Plural Happiness

A curtain bellying like a pregnant cloud, warm white
light refracted through a tumbler of peat-smoked scotch—
a scorcher of a day at cooling end, with stupendous berries
to eat in lieu of supper, the scoffed pint box of blueberries
chased by a half of cantaloupe & Maytag blue cheese
spread across the remains of last night's baguette—
a plural happiness—I feel encouraged for all
within range—even the hang-gliding error that sent
Jesus spiraling down to earth seems a commitment.
Tomorrow we'll go to Alison's wedding, who
at age 2 & 3/4 attended our wedding 26 years ago,
her blond curls a mystery to be held up & photographed
between her mother & father dark-haired Diane & Larry—
in the riddle of our recessive genes once in a while
something surprising waits for anybody out & about.
Like hearing for the first time a blind preacher or waking
in a Gros Vent campground south of Jenny Lake,
the best happiness is always accidental,—& why not?
I was going to say something about boundlessness
back there (or was it getting gassed I meant?), but that
isn't it exactly either. Tho it is pretty close. Close
enough. And real. Real enough, & sure. God it felt good
to heat water on a primus stove while yawning
and to wash my face in cold Gros Vent & love Michaela.

Forehead

I love you
I know as much as anything
for your courage
so companionably invisible
as it is
that it passes mostly
as simple
good sense. I don't mean you're
practical at all—god forbid—
only persistent
as far as dying brothers & cold calls
are concerned—not violent,
not weak, but like a lantern afloat on a wave
open if necessary
to sinking your light
offshore. Onshore
I am as you would know
strongly sometimes
impatient & inside a swarm of loud thoughts
self-absorbed & locked-up.
If you were to die
who would remove me
from those thoughts?
When you lean your forehead
against mine
what you hear inside there
are all those
sounds likely, vibrations
like windowpanes rattled by headland squalls
or bullet trains
late forever & loaded down
with passengers green

as hoodie-wearing witches.
I lean my forehead against
your forehead
gently knowing both
will shortly vanish.
"First of all," says
Virgil, "find
a protected place
for the bees
to make their
honey, a place that's
safe from wind."

Dog Sled Dawn

Simone Rivard Michaela Sullivan
David Rivard *en famille*
speaking to you, Sam Walker dying—
walking by your house,
what's that in the rain? Your sign
advises victors, I mean it warns
visitors, *watch out, railing broken*—
your handrail rinkadink aluminum,
and it's cracked, & the door it
heads to is painted purple, *Tahitian Plum*
the Sherwin-Williams Co. calls it—
Dog Sled Dawn perhaps
the tag you'd have
loved. *Watch out*—I get
it, Sam—in lieu of
hexagram wisdom, in lieu
of divination via cooling entrails,
pony shadow, runes, green
tea leaves in drag, jellied turtle, or
squirrel tracks—I get it, totally—
ask for no promises, go this way
carefully, serve your people, be
cheerful, ample, feel increasingly
forgiving if incapable of being
heroic, be heroic, so far as that goes.

Pirated Music

2856 Kbps the download speed

 —& tho there is no scot-free, & comparisons are odious,
all you have to do it would seem
     is ask
to hear the music, & you shall—

  what life better than a festival of file-swap networks
  where amateur bootleggers can cheat
  the talent of their livelihood, of breakfast & a mattress?

 As for compensation for
bespoke trumpet players & faux-black vocals draped in snakeskin,
    shuffle on, it says,

if you're on your way to the gym via Amy Winehouse, Miles
  in Europe "Round Midnight" 1959, & the one about a sailor's ghost
run off with the house carpenter's wife, a lovesick mother of three

  —"Are those the cliffs of Spain, my love?"—no, but

later, reading on the train, I'll cross a cloudburst of sailboats
  mostly Sunfish in the demanding wind & Apache-Dancer's fog
    of the river basin—the mothball gold
dome of the statehouse up on the hill, red-lined Delmonico & Courvoisier
  specials for state reps from Fitchburg & West Roxbury
in Bowdoin Street chop-houses—

  "happy when I am alone & not myself"—

 I wish I had written that,

can almost hear those words as mine & not Tom Clark's.

Saul Bellow Nevertheless

And the older, more inscrutable codes
we lived by are dispersing now
disappearing
nevertheless certain characters
and episodes said
to have vanished long ago go on holding out
in all our history books—
the Fugitive Slave Law
Whiskey Rebellion
and chanted Diamond Sutra trailing
in pursuit of well-pursued Casey Jones,
or Nader's Raiders
and the Peabody Coal Company
with its High Sheriff
Cotton Mather
handed on in school
to the youngest
stakeholders. With their brief lives
lived in rotation
as they age they recall only a few
of those facts, the face of a dogged instigator
Tolstoy de Gaulle or Clay (either Cassius or Henry)
may return to them
while riding aboard a crowded commuter train,
its regulated speed
neither fatal or ponderous
tho for a time they feel its lurching
in their legs after arrival,
come to that city full of laughter but ferocious in springtime,
where some try hard simply to be good
some to be arrogant, enchanted, vital, cruel—
Senator X draped in a paper bib by his dental hygienist
cross-dressers in shawls
a teacher with Finnish mustache off to a mathematics drill

alongside a kind geographer—
and on what one of them wishes was All Soul's Day
of all days a crowd
of what seem to be crack counters roam the sidewalk,
looking down at the ground under their feet,
as if trying to avoid
the morning headline—*Saul Bellow Dead*—
in spite of the hand-blocked high-crowned & featherless
slate gray fedora pictured on his head
Saul Bellow is dead,
and the Kit-Kat girl
whose downstream tabloid this is,
an ambitious red-headed Southie
4-months pregnant in tweed stretch pants loitering
at the Starbucks pick-up counter,
as she goes on staring at this photo of him
she feels almost
sure she remembers the face of this Bellow
from the cover of a paperback
in the house of some boy whose lips she kissed just once
in 10th grade,
chapped lips.

1968

The thought of a red-tailed hawk hang-glides mid-air
above the roar of a stadium crowd, a 5th inning stand-up
triple two RBI's on a handheld transistor radio a week
after Robert Kennedy the doomed thane had died
—the idea of getting the idea & getting it right at last
had accompanied him you might say from morning to night,
long travels made aboard chartered aircraft & trains.
Those of us whose names will never be found in either
footnotes or headlines, we heard the sound too of plates
and utensils being gathered up amid thunder clouds
far-away but stained the delicate purple of cone flowers
by lightning seen all of a sudden from the parish picnic—
our laying down together after shedding our sweatshirts
having just taken place—& the confusion just beginning
for those of us who felt ourselves immune or weightless,
peaceful, without wickedness— those who at first had
failed to spot how the creek drank the cradle or tried to
before spitting it out near the Quonset hut—the baby's
mother very, very white & a bit twee later under
the grapevines & feeling hidden if not by broad leaves
and shade then by the dream of over-ripe grapes
musky & sharpened in cool air at the bottom of her mind—
the rest of us feeling betrayed, but betrayed by whom?

Vigorish

The exorbitant devils of a showery late July day
brew up a potential cure in the heathen sweetness
of lavender—but who heals as he used to?
2 weeks after a hike across hills of heavy scrub
long scratches still scab my legs—a kind of vigorish paid
for abundant living. You pay as you go. Mornings
at this point are either like spread sails or (more likely)
spread-sheets—they fill fast. Mornings are fortunes,
but as suspect as a wristwatch running backward.
Would I really want to live counter-clockwise?—
and circling back to when exactly?—I made my mother
laugh today by saying I saw visions out my 2nd grade
classroom like Blake's fiery angels in Howdy-Doody
sleepwear. I must have seen something, always
staring out those high windows, much to my teacher
Sister Rae Anne's epic consternation—2 or 3 times
she summoned my father to the principal's office
to complain about my "episodes of distraction."
Then gave up. She wasn't a very good teacher,
but already I was avid for what could be learned best
from cloud shadow frying on a hot rectory roof
or maybe an air raid siren at noon. Later, in high school,
the Jesuits made clear the sinister nature of both
doubt & faith. They were both thuggish
and enlightened, & a red-haired one claimed once
that while we need most to be saved none of us
could understand what we desire to be saved
from—tho if our luck held, he said, at some point
the need would simply vanish. They ran a tight ship.

Crush

Self-contained smile of a free & roomier girl, Catholic school
Gail McDermott seen as a Scots-Irish wanderer in 8th grade math class,
her untucked 14 year-old hair like salty palisades-blond wind,
and once later, after college, at 23 seen again at a house party
she wore toreador pants like Carmen post-cigar factory—
no soccer girl with flat butt, & certainly not in Kate Moss territory
but thin, with very white & ardent teeth, stubborn
kind eyes, talking of Brad her brother, & social work.
Stopwatched in this world amid party chatter & dance music
for 15 minutes, 39 seconds I felt everything I had felt
for her in middle school then—charmed, itinerant, slap-happy, & razed—
rewound to fantasies of petting in the class cloakroom during gym.
I wish her picture had been taken there on that second floor
stairway by some semi-professional from another era—
Jacques-Henri Lartigue of the Cote d'Azur perhaps, now
he was someone who knew how slow learning is, & how good,
even if it is sad that our clothing goes out of style so fast.
Would I like to speak with her again? Not actually, no,
but I would have liked to have come upon her photo in a book
and thought of her as she may be idling in a black SUV
waiting now for a daughter perhaps a pick-up at a ballet studio
after practice in the October twilight clean-looking
in his long white smock the barber keeps stepping over
to his shop window to peek out at her, harmless, instantly shy.

Working Black

The part of Stockholm I saw at 22, I saw as an employee & thief
more or less—an American sweating in clogs & kitchen whites—
booster of those clogs from a Gamla Stan stall, a shoplifter
of Icelandic sweaters, book thief—*Gravity's Rainbow, Justine*—
I worked day-shifts as scullery boy for Claes & Eva at the restaurant
Hos Oss, pot scrubber, peeler of turnips & potatoes, blade sharpener—
"working black" the Swedes said, meaning for most foreigners
off-the-books & untaxed, the welfare state scammed, meaning
for others that you had vanished, you were a Vera or a Paulo
or Damishi who had fled from your home in some southern dictatorship
fearful that you might be "disappeared," so perhaps you no longer
existed anymore, or didn't deserve to. "If people believe,"
Berndt had said, "it's only because they wish for themselves to see,"
tho the chef was speaking of having had the dead appear to him
as bewildering presences, travelers trapped on the blank screen
of his broken television, souls stored in a paranormal peepshow.
Meanwhile I mopped tiles or whisked a bowl of whipped cream
as the middle-management of Gulf Oil drifted over
from a nearby office tower for pea soup & thick pancakes & jam
every Thursday lunch—there was a sad gentility & boredom
sunk deep in the witch-hazel faces of these sober businessmen,
far from the tripping & mobilizations of dumbstruck America
1975. Faces unlike my own bearded & baffled face.
What is the taste of raw potato in a steamy northern kitchen?—
the iron earthiness of your mother & father outgrown, left behind.

And Then

Then the sunrise comes on piecemeal & cold-blooded—
vesper bells & the rotation of wind farm blades, axels
turning in a haz-mat haze high above the scramble
of technicians & crew chiefs—because the wind
like the spirit isn't exiled here, it chooses this world,
and must partake of risks as well as wonder, must
agree to touch here & there every swollen little
fleabite & every helium-filled balloon, every
dining car & bright hothouse, each haunted moth,
every Baedeker & bit of nocturnal gunk.
Years ago the great convoys steamed away to war,
one behind the other, the ships eager to cast a vote
for conquest & empire. Now seasoned wood smoke
burns on a beach spectral in the ancestral sunlight.
And anger still leaves its taste in every mouth.
Even on Delos, where Apollo was born. And in Helsinki,
at the lake preferred by redheads. Or on a glide
path over Sapporo. So even on the island of Delos
adjustments will need to be made to set free the day—
simple acts, like walking bare-foot across beach stones
so the small boats called *kaiki* can be launched again
on the warm waters of some secluded cove despite
worrisome sunspots & thanks to the immediate need
of a few aging men & women to get back to the water,
the very bay they once swam naked, the plankton
on fire every night in August. Happiness is still there.

To Answer

the purity of rain clouds
with the purity of a greengrocer in an ankle-length apron,
or one purity with another—

        a Tibetan's gold-capped eye tooth
        answered once & for all by a floor-show breakfast, a plateful
        of double-sauced eggs, a brioche—

to balance the fury of
our collective amnesia with a compassion
for Catholic guilt—

in the Age of the Absolute Cell, to answer the variability of our genes
with the wingspan of an Adirondack summer,

        to match the purity of beehives with the purity of houseboats
        and the onset of cancer with an over-fished sea;

to reply to a movie in a darkened living room
                      (our breathing in time with a dogged actor),
to answer an afternoon of forgivable horoscopes
or the civic morning's haunted prince, to answer his assassination,
to answer the crunch time of tearoom waiters or the chanting of pilgrims
        or all of the above
with an hour of singing—

(because some blues singers should play opera houses, no?)—

nonetheless, I'm not sure if anyone alive could identify
a purity talented-enough to answer *this* black rock—
                in the middle of the coffee shop, this aunt
speaking to a miserable teenage girl, leaning in to tell her,
"Well, I hope your therapy isn't going to dredge up a lot of awful things
from childhood, no one
should have to go over that stuff in their mind."

It's unworthy of an answer.

        A signal fire is
worth it, a toothache in your heel
is, & the trustiness of a sleeping servant;

                        nonetheless,
this black rock will not be answered.

It

"Anodyne lingerie" was Amy Dryansky's
way of describing it. "The sufferers of giganticism
are out in the fog with their mallets," wrote
David Blair. Meaning what Snyder meant perhaps
by "spring-water in the green creek is clear,"
a crib from Han Shan. Meaning otherwise
"trouble no more," as sung by Sister Rosetta Tharpe
or "now it's your turn, mister!"—as any babysitter might say—
even if it is unquestionably true that no one should ever
promise anything so vague & huge—a youngish
woman with a macaroon talking to a toddler,
her voice the galvanic bath it all floats in. *It*. All of it.
"Solitude, my mother, tell me my life again,"
wrote the uncle of Czeslaw Milosz last time he saw it.
A blissful state of mind, or an anxiety attack. It
has a need to be called by its rightful name
or explained because it can't see itself clearly,
plus is terribly changeful. In any case, "Grazie" is
still the best way to say good-bye to it. And it wasn't fooled
when my brother referred to it as a "piece of cake."
Perhaps the best advice ever given about it can be found
in these lines by a sadly late & formerly high-wattage
earthling: "When you come to something," he said,
"stop to let it pass, so you can see what else is there."
"It's murder," my doctor likes to say, & it is,
but it still wants you to love it back. My mother
dealt with it by telling the four of us, me, my
brother & two sisters, "go ahead, do whatever
you want." By which she meant we should do
exactly what she thought best. As if that should
have put it to rest. Thankfully, it did not. *Grazie.*

To Simone

Now that your hair your dark brown
and slightly coppery hair at 11 so like your mother's
hair falls well past your shoulders when wet
pasted to the back of your t-shirt after a shower
as you sit at the top of the stairs laughing
instructed by the storm of some unlimited unseen feeling
I remember that when you were younger
and some passerby or friend said how beautiful you were
(which was & is true) I would nod simply
tho the custom might have been to thank them
for the compliment I thought at the time
it was dumb to take undeserved credit for what
seemed an obvious indebtedness to happenstance
(I mean the wanderings of DNA across the many powers
of heated summer skin thankful for oxygen kisses & wine)
and sometimes I even thought it might make as much sense
if I said "all aboard" in reply or "be careful that match is lit"
or "she is the stone drenched with rain that marks the way"
but I didn't & feel sure you would be relieved at that
in light of your very sensible desire (and one that we share)
to fly above or walk atop or run over or sit upon as much earth
as is possible without having to suffer an embarrassment
of any sort & at any rate you were never there exactly
when someone said "she's beautiful" you were nearby
it's true & within earshot but far away
in the folklore & gossip of play paying no attention at all
to the adult world now you're moving closer to it
yourself almost ready (or not) the first warm day in May—
believe in what you feel
never to be abandoned
elsewhere tonight
the thief with a branch of our climbing white rose in her hand
does too.

Somewhere between a Row of Traffic Cones
and the Country Once Called Burma

A word I can't remember
some blackhawk of a word flew out of you
at uninsurable speed
but with a 4th grade pitch & intonation to it
it sounded something like *instinctual*
tho wasn't—
it must have surprised me so as to give me amnesia—
and where did that come from
I wondered
what pay master always on the lookout
in your mind
for the next expanse of empty skyline
had handed over
that orphaned bit of heat lightning?—
I smiled at you then
as one smiles at the stranger seated across an airplane aisle
in the shuddering of the cabin
having to trust temporarily the larger
and more complex machinery
hurrying its corporate logo through the wind shear
between Boston & Atlanta—
I mean, who exactly
were you then so oblivious in your strength
and eating corn on the cob
and grilled lamb & rice
and drinking cold milk—
sweet fragile trance state of a late family supper,
we had been sitting there
on the back porch discussing the sentencing of Martha Stewart—
she deserved it,
you had just said—coolly, flatly—with an almost baleful shrug
and none of your usual
smiles or tentative trademark drowsiness—

this is an oxygen
cracked open by glimmerings
I thought,
and you are more set free
than we ever were—
a street away a row of fender-scuffed traffic cones
glowed brighter in the dusk
while on the other side of the world
in the country that was once called Burma
a moth seemed to be trapped within a circle of burning grass—
and it was in the area between these two places
that the word leapt out of you
just then
whatever it was
insouciant indisputable incorrigible inhabitable ink blot.

Wandering Oxygen

Exactly what the future holds
as advertised
only occasionally can anyone say—
I mean, if a friend comes by
to ask you *what's*
for dinner?
and you tell her *mussels over pasta*
isn't it mussels & linguini
when her plate turns up
of late?—
then the mussels taste sweet,
the pasta that's been prepped with
squid ink pretty near *al dente,*
the summer evening
a crush of garlic
brilliancy of lemon zest—

and as we sit there the table
wobbles
like a somewhat excitable thought, & it goes on
wobbling if nudged
by any summer-made adult—
a table on a wooden deck not
too high above the charismatically
rowdy Atlantic—
what a lot
of smiling gin & tonic talk!
with a vast string
of plovers sliding by, & the string snapping
down & back,
and the birds wandering
in oxygen, then belting out
toward the cove
whenever some
child wet behind the ears
shouts.

Slightly More Alone

You want to know
which of these it might be
better to possess?—
a blond cloak of pelican softness?
or a pair of black shoes
and eyeglasses of the sort
handed out each & every
election day to any damned
voter in Vicksburg not
"born with Buddha's eye
south of Mason-Dixon"?

You poor sad thing
with your master class
and shaved whiskers,
while you slurped that last
slug of soda everything changed
and in the lives of petty thieves
everywhere it seems important
now to feel so hidden
as to be a broken arrow
or downed Piper Cub fallen
somehow to the floor of someone's
sadly stubborn heart.

Let the Cabbies Come Fetch Us Now

Light rain & mist on all the noises
I get back to

not far from the footbridge held there
in the air above the river

by the light of streetlamps (or so it had seemed
just a few minutes ago)

while I'd crossed it soaked & full of adrenaline.
Everyone's gaga here, you might say,

but none of us really
likes the rotisserie light of noon,

not unless it comes across
privatized by rain—

So after a while
I went for a walk, like whatever needed to be decided

could be
decided without me—

As tho beyond
the crouching rain clouds there were a steadier

hemisphere sheltering
somewhere to the west—

the place more or less
where the river picks up its look, that mercury-poured-over-a-belly

look—maybe a stone's throw
from Green Street—kind-of-charismatic Green Street—

a lucky road—
Van Morrison & Michael Palmer lived there

in 1968, unknown
to one another—

and what a marvelous bit of factual
taffeta that would be

if I weren't so afraid of waking up
shaken by rebuke. You don't get it,

she said, you don't
understand what I've been going through

this year. Like her doubt had
in mind some trip

still incomplete. I wanted someone
to help. As if it were

possible for
some voice not

hers or mine just
then to say

let the cabbies come fetch us now.

Coffeehouse, Eastern Standard Time

"Do you think your cat is capable
          of non-judgment & unconditional
love, like a higher power
          is?—maybe God reaches out
through your cat—multiply that
          times a billion, that's
the power of God. They broke
          the mold, they say. I say
not only did they break the mold,
          they also beat the hell
out of the mold-maker. . . ."—He spoke
          non-stop—a rehab
counselor from the motherless
          halfway-house—spoke
to a boy-like man only recently
          made sober by heart-attack
in sunlight, two teeth missing,
          a chimneysweep & methadone
clinic habitué in shamrock-
          green warm-up jacket
the Celtics licensed. Compassion,
          yes, & care, for a moment
they were there in me, then
          gone just as
quickly, like a lightship
          accelerating off-course
after slipping its anchorage cable.
          Don't believe poetry—
poetry, which would use metaphor
          to give grace
to the grief of everyday
          homemade human failure,
indifference. As if words had no
          weight, & didn't accumulate

in you. Poetry? The evidence is skimpy,
        and I wouldn't want
my daughter to have to carry
        the tonnage of my coffin
with her hands. Now, check
        this out for me—a young
dad lifts a screaming
        toddler to plunk his arching
seal-like body into the wretched
        high chair, while two
years older his calm brother
        shows off by counting to 8.
What prepares us best
        for life? Years later,
which of these boys will understand
        better why some hand
has taken magic-marker
        to scrawl a single word
on the tiled men's room wall,
        there, right above
the urinal, one word, & one
        word only: "usurp."

Double Elegy, with Curse

Reagan dead this Saturday the last—

    the falsifying mind cratered,
    the brain that was a salt block America loved to lick—

but Ray Charles struck down
yesterday outlasts him
by three days forever now—

    the basic blues chord
    a power of the arisen—

to the Lord's child
betrayed by lightless waves comes recompense
and cleansing tides;

to the Lord's child
comes late-night baths with a supper-club waitress,
and fingernails soaked in brine—

the basic blues chord
a power
of the arisen, swaying & sweaty bodies of the
sweating, ever-blinking,
and chain-smoking choir
as they stand there in their pews—

    the faithful kneel in any country church
    and pray,

they give thanks for the water
and to the name within the water
that their threadbare maker made damn sure
to pour upon their faces—

but the rooster-cheeked comptrollers
the war-gamed & prosecutorial arrive by limos
black as shivering crows they are the untrue
and carry home a bright evil—

not innocent I hope
they'll all be dead soon
in my mind too.

Something That You'll Never Know
Can Hurt the Quiet of a Sunday Morning

The swale still green the river runs
and stirred by a truck's engine
the cabin's roof a roof of unpainted
sheet metal blinds the sun in June
among the slender birches
it blinds as always the pine
the corporal sits against crying
home as he is once more
it blinds the crow that's flying by
and then the river
so that the river fog in turn whitens
that grassy field where the sled dogs ran
a few month's ago
the corporal's mother recalls
some of the dogs as they rushed along yelping
here & there in the snow
their paws had shed the threadbare booties
they wore like socks hand-sewn for them
out of corduroy scraps
by the owner of the pulp mill their master.
When the child returns for good at first
there's a happiness in the house.
But the army barber who each week
had cut the boy's hair there
in that desert half a world away
he walks this morning amid rebel rain
hearing its amen & refusing to shout.

What We Call Childhood

What we call childhood isn't
what a child would call it—
so she doesn't speak
of how she was the most sensitive girl in the convent school kindergarten
or that the god who was a panhandler
wore a fly's face
and that whenever he dawdled beneath the striped
awning of the shop selling cut-rate shoes & her class
had to walk by him as it happened
on the way to the public library
she would cling to her teacher then & cry
steered off by the old nun's fingers, she doesn't mention
why her bedspread changed to blue
each July, the sky lighter blue, the screen door green, her stepfather's
beach house having been rehabbed under the influence of sea light,
sea light & contractor kickbacks, she doesn't
say she was
a girl by the first week of 6th grade summer vacation well-known
as a primitive freelancer whenever she rode her old 3-speed English racer
handless downhill to the anchorage;
none of it gets talked about, certainly
not the angora sweater
and the Chinatown bracelets
or those evenings
3 winters later when she danced in front of her bedroom mirror
with headphones on & always inside of the sight lines
because she was wearing blue bracelets
and somehow that
had given her the idea to break into the empty summer cottages
with her rustbelt boyfriend; she doesn't even
say she liked how her legs got long
in a kick-pleat skirt but hated her dark hair
for curling if it threatened rain—
and likewise

her whole childhood—she doesn't talk about it—
so it's all kept in play,
and no one will ever feel free to tell her what it was worth,
not even on that autumn moor
where against all odds a narrow sandy road
gleams at midnight.

Lay It Down

And it's only common sense
but they say that over the ache
of a disappointment or happiness so pure
that it makes you stammer
if you wanted to you could put on a seasonal perfume
and a dress as tight around your thighs & as self-involved
as a cloud arranged
to hover above a tentative
blue lake
and even if it were purchased off-the-rack
such a silhouette
when worn near one particular black-green pine would
tend to make of you a will-less
and absolutely scavenging wind
so long as you were to lean there
deep among the tossing pines,
ankles darkened by road dust & sun—
and so you do,
so you blow around my cabin door
and through the monstrous throat of a mockingbird,
the killer tongue of wakefulness,
the strep throat of stung whistles
and spilled pills.

To Lynda Hull

The biographical is boring tho
you tried
to refute this by charging language with currents
streaming into back-lit
gentian-colored chiffon, seraphically shabby
hotel rooms, ruinous taxi rides, Puerto Rican transvestites,
jailhouse conversions, brocades, & mah-jongg tiles.

And even if it sounds heroic
there was no real drama in the way
I carried you over my shoulder
and into the emergency room one September night—
it's a trick called the fireman's hoist

and was taught by a diligent father
to his two sons
in the hope that if necessary
it might be of use
one day.

It was.

Before they pumped the drugs from your stomach
with a concoction of emetics & pharmaceutical charcoal
the on-duty resident asked
what meds you might have taken—

everything, I said.

Reality is sometimes as clear-cut as that.

You survived,
tho I can't claim to have saved you—

you died on a dark road
months later & several weeks
after Simone was born—

but there's something I would like to confess—

I was a little afraid your
spirit might enter my daughter then.

There was a square of thrift-store fabric
you'd brought to us a few panels of worn quilt coverlet
a scrap of disintegrating energies.

Why else would you have given it
to mark her birth?—
it seemed a remnant of your life
wishing to be transferred,

so I put it where it still is
at the bottom of the cedar chest,
a place where it would not be destroyed
but its energies contained
at rest.

That (as you would say) was very Rivard,
and, yes, silly & superstitious,

tho cedar is still used for coffins & small boats both
common means of transport.

The Question inside Tuesday

You might say
it's just an answer, this bee—
and even if

as could hardly
be believed it happens
at this instant

to have flown
from a woman's hair
(Michaela's),

it's still
every bit as here as
she is, in

public, as this
place (the Broadway Market)
is public,

its
baked goods counter Tuesday morning
busy. You might

also say that
the cup the bee floats
above

is
the question—a cold, soul-
conducting

cup of what
can only be called
orphan's milk.

All the Way from Murasakino

Awake at 5:18, & happy
it's possible
to touch your hair—neither too shy or too late—

my eyes opening
out of a dream
like the hero reproached & homeless

there
because the vengeful branch librarian,
ticked-off by sloppy filing

at the circulation desk, & pitiless,
stone-faced, she'd stood watch over me
en route to

Vancouver, the sky above the fishing trawler
flat-out muggy
as rain fell through a turpentine haze

all the way from Murasakino,
that field violet
in Kyoto a thousand years ago—

not exactly lost,
I couldn't find my life—baffled
by an amnesia like

a well-intentioned
loneliness (itself a gift I'd gave myself)—
when we docked, I was

let go, & only
felt someone might tell me if I could make
my way again, further,

heading far inland,—
and that's when I woke—then,
then saw

your hair
inches from my face on the pillow—
all these years

we've had together
ahead of us once more, time starting up, so
to speak,

and so glad
I was going all the way
there, with you.

Birthday

Squirrel's nest high in the swacked bare tree,
Norwegian maple, I guess—
right!—& all those long dark daughter & wife hairs
clumped in our bathtub drain—

and in the mirror
this is me now, at 50—
my face—tho it's altered
into some mother's father's father's, my
mother's, in fact—big forehead
now that you mention it.

My face was licked at birth,
a long time back.

But what to ask of the world today?

Lost time will not come again.
Summer-sunned-on, tanned faces
will come, of course,

but so will Joan's dim & rainy June—

What to ask for then?

I hope for
just enough jeopardy, tho not the cold kind
of my own making. Occasional clarity
would be nice too, even if it isn't always
of my own mind's
motion. Not to be baffled
by thinking power is real. Mostly,

I hope to keep my arms & legs strong
(so as to hold on to certain lovely others)—

hello, Michaela & Simone!

Note to Myself

Having survived self-
esteem (both low & high), like
surfacing

out of a to-do
list for civil war
in the heart—

Having
been a back-stabber (when said
back was my own), or

lucky Darwinian
holder of
the Ace of Spades,

in my mind—
Getting to see myself
as a green midge

or
as a pine tree looming like
a fetching samurai

at the edge
of a meadow—I get a little
tired—& strangely

everywhere I go
seems one
step closer to wherever I

thought
I was when I left for
wherever I thought

I wanted to be.
Given the round
ranginess of earth, always

thinking of myself—tho
that's it for me now. Enough. No
more, thank you. No, really.

Nostalgia

What to do now with the nostalgia for first handjobs
there in the house
of the Adamsville doctor
if at the time
it was Mott the Hoople & T. Rex playing on the stereo at low volume
and pharmaceutically-fueled
a young woman & man sprawled out stoned
in front of the fireplace
coincidentally happy in their alive white underwear
while the children
she babysat slept in the bedrooms above?
What to do with
the pillow waiting to be real
near her head? What to do with the jerky
pumping of her hand
certainly awkward
compared to those things his own could do
but better by far let's face it
what's better than skin evolving & arriving imprecisely
at an exploded attention span
if someone else is helping? That was an easy lesson,
and afterward he had liked
the way she'd wiped her hand on his leg.
What to do tho with the next day
and how it seemed then
that the best part of the river was its reassembling under a bright sun,
its makeshift waves & flattering untroubled aura
looking forward to the accelerations of a rain squall
and for Frances to be sentenced
six months later to a term of three years probation
even tho under no explicit threat
she'd tried to return the scrips she'd pocketed from the doctor's desk?

What to do with that oak desk & its dark green blotter?
Or else maybe it isn't
a problem? Maybe it doesn't
need to be solved?

Pasted Up in the Vicinity of the Sun

Not to be infinite
despite the child you once were,
not to be every iota of every vengeful comedian in the world,
and never to be the entirety of a trash fish
never the agility of a stag
or its molecular structure extant,
never to be the nursery maid a-gossiping in bright light
nor a dusting of white baking flour,
and not to be everyone's absolutely informed consent
and all the threads in every V-neck in the world,
and likewise not to be all the raffia involved
in each & every sector of the planet's raffia trade
and the bow wave from an aircraft carrier
and the superfluous pathos
of the fleas hidden beneath a leaf,
never to be a leaf fallen from a catalpa
never the Aqua Velva girl
never the scavenger gods
and my galley charging with forgetfulness
and the jury foreman's veins
and a brace of well-oiled pistols
and Luanawahai Pond,
never to be the mortally dark loves floating in a moat
and not one of the specks of white flour
thirty-six in all fallen from a baguette of sourdough bread
for the sole
purpose of being identified in error as anthrax,
never to be the anthrax spread atop a marble bank counter,
never to be a scavenger god in Blue Hills, Maine,
not always to be David Rivard
not to be Rachel Nardin
never to be Tomaz Salamun
never to be Mike Mayo
never to be Monica Navarro

not ever Solomon Burke
and in particular
never ever to be Johnny Barrels—
not to be infinite
but to struggle to flow through the lock like air
instead of as a key.

How Else to Say It

And the guilt that must be got rid of
all one's life
how does my neighbor feel about that?
these appearing but feckless days
vain or proud
with riverine lavender & lupine in hand
a true lion of Judah is what
he is
while waiting for a light snow cover
and insulin
there's slush on his G-Unit sneakers
muffin crumbs on his scarf
an aging incendiary
cosmopolitan but unfussy
back from an early morning Mass
and Holy Communion.

How else to say it
except that it's not such a bad way to make a living
bringing home
some sign as unshakeable as ashes
on this particular Ash Wednesday's forehead
the quiet clear reminder of a smudged thumbprint
above his eyes
but in those eyes
a shine like the feeling inexplicable
to anyone lacking the sweet understanding
of a dog in boyhood
that to pee against the mossed bark of Juniper pine
is to be real in your soul.

Townie Gossip (Since You Asked)

Green leaves of maples tarred silver with mist
and on the clothesline a camisole billowing in a breeze stuffed
with jonquils over there behind the rooming house
where Sheila's brushing back her dripping hair & talking birth control
and giggling to herself about recycling bins & reincarnation at birth,
a wry smile on her face
as a keyless car lock chirps twice
and the whole city seems to lift then out of a footprint,
all of it timed impeccably
for a break in the clouds—swinging blue sky, open door—

a sensational minute or two
to live through all in all,
abundant with the smells only a century
like this could cook-up, the avenue & its wisps of dieseled air aching
with the fragrance of lilacs,
and none of it asking in return
for sustained applause or your signature on a loyalty oath.
An almost prehistoric
pleasure. Contentment in transit. A bravura
with streaming audio. A bonus.
And shareable. Because bad luck comes
whenever time begins
to limit itself to you, & good luck is largely
reciprocal, & mostly roving, & in the Riverside taverns
at neap tide
the leather jobbers & print-shop foremen bent
over Buds & frosted schooners of India Pale Ale & jiggers of Seagram's
they value clarity over irony, a slightly buzzed clarity,
townie gossip over metropolitan chic.

A modesty rules the neuromuscular pathways
at times such as these,

but no one raises a hand to ask permission either.
There are homes inside of this—

and that's the whole story—there are homes here—

      & simplicity isn't always a defect or disguise,

      & we don't always have to live behind the scenes.

Churrascaria

Your breathing calm,
as if all suffering could be explained
by a plastic bull, a steer risen up on hind hooves, no slouch
but big as a short granddad or a tallish child of spry mischievous bearing,
nicked horns, stout smile, stout chest & belly
attired in black waiter's vest & starched white apron

outside the restaurant, a Brazilian *churrascaria* painted
red & black the team colors of *Clube do Recife* futbol—
"all the meat you can eat"
on the menu this really quite friendly bull
stands there clutching—all suffering explained.

Explained away? No—
because to be deluded would ruin the day.

Is This?

Wanting to believe justice is at least possible,
not naïve, not plunder & bribery dusted with confectioner's sugar,
no cover for crimes
in the name of democracy as war & market share—

another week in the era of rendition & methamphetamine bathtubs—

uneasy,

because I want to believe myself innocent, somewhat
(a human need, not an unforgivable demand), would consider
my country decent, or curable, as it seems
sometimes it might be
that the laughter is not coming from chuckleheads, oblivious, the outcome
has not betrayed the dream, the gift not turned ruthless—
but why should anyone have to
tell this
to a daughter anyway?—
                          & so is this place our country
evil now? & what are we? a nation of
self-absorbed gravediggers beery with grief for those they've buried?
    (and as we bury more)
vengeful & suspicious, rancorous, flipped-out,
or are we a shadow kingdom, like a colony of wood lice in a fallen elm
    full of the indifference of appetite,
or perhaps we're merely dazed?
baffled by the demands of our dreamlike good intentions
    and hurt
by a world that sees us at worst
as a malevolent apparition & at best as a smoke-free zone
ideal for the production of flash-frozen meat patties.

All the Same

All the same, since she's just swapped out the splinter
in her index finger for a flash of November lightning
the widowed hairdresser walks the dusty road to town,
soapy pine needles clinging to her black skirt
and vest. You watched her in the movie you watched
last night. Vendettas at sea & in a not-so-sober
schoolyard, but a candy-coated wind off the bay.
The disgraced biologist now a slaughterhouse
butcher with breaking & entering on his mind.
A tavern. A man & woman meet, each believing
the other to be of higher rank. A bonfire later
by a river-ford, & a close-up of Italian eyebrows
and high summer cheekbones. That was last night.
Today, calm, all the silence you missed out on
while you were so busy being you the last few weeks.
And Scotch broom in bloom, tiny yellow flowers riding
lightly atop sunlight's most enthusiastic freakazoid.

Manny Ramirez

Flaky, but sometimes somber & steroidally corn-rowed,
Manny Ramirez rounds the bases now to high fives & fist bumps.

 His dark dreads, his whacked
attention span (except at bat),

 & pitch identification skills to die for
 (like Renée Fleming, but with a heftier entourage)—

 it's all a floor show
to the tax accountants, his agents & handlers
Ivy frat monkeys like the young lawyers
with bottle-blond sundresses in tow three rows behind the dugout—

 man, you got to put your ball cap on backward
 pretty early in the morning to buy
 advisors better than these smart boys,

 even if their women are bored stiff—

the girls' lipstick strained through your intelligence would stain it
 algebraically pink—

 but who knows what Ramirez wonders about there inside his head?

because an open-ended inquiry goes on
constantly in that glamorous cul-de-sac of his,

 as it does for each of us, of course—

inside the ballpark at any given moment
it's clear that in
any number of minds there are enough questions to make
a miracle
out of all our faces,

a miraculous cloud (an essential & virtuoso cloud of changefulness)
such as the one that surrounds Section 22, Row P, Seat 3—

                                        except, maybe all
                        our questions are only one question really?—

"What could I do to make my mother happy?"

Bantam Tricycle

A 3-year-old's
ringing a bell on the handlebar
of his rusty bantam

trike—you don't
say?—how nice to learn the
thumb

has an opposable power—
so the phone
too can be put down

after calling
your mother—seriously,
her claims for

genetic superiority
at 78 a surprised pride & nervous
laughter, grateful,

anxious, a bit
guilty she's better off than
many she sees adrift

on canes & walkers, friends'
far-traveling brainwaves arrested, those
whose bodies

betrayed them so
they look so 87 ten years ahead
of time winding

down—I hope I
don't wake in a later part of my
life either embarrassed

by the view
or struck dumb, lame, and
blind—not that

I'm always in touch
with sights & sounds around me
as it is—tho

I would like
to be, more
alive—

we think we
know the cards we are
dealt, but do we?

Teacher

Everything, you said, *is too brief,*
eternal, stable, unpredictable. Everything
could always be taken away, & would—

        & has been, now that you are dead.

      To live inside the moods of another
not yourself
was always your wish—to be greeted by friends,
& inscrutable to yourself.

      Some night will be the last I'll dream of you, Jon—

even if you have always drawn nearer
in dreams—charming & spry—but often a little shaky
or dazed—the cheery survivor
of some grand mal car wreck.

Where will you go then? If you ride
through the town of Presbyterian Church
as the halfhearted gunfighter
dies in a drift
will the snow that falls there
still look Japanese? Where are you, teacher?

Wishes

"I had the wish to be changed,"
sang the tentmaker St. Paul that night,

arriving as he had at last
in my dream of drinking by the dam—

but as this was the night
of the day of the downward-burning ladders

I kept to the towpath a little longer,
this time bypassing the bathhouse,

wondering if I had wanted to
what it would feel like

to open its blue door & be reborn,
as wary as any

immigrant wearing white ear buds—
later

the one most often referred to
as the Blind Sheikh,

he said a force would be sent soon
to terrorize & punish all

of the occupiers in their homes—
not a wish—

the sun shone
around the edges of a spring umbrella,

a certain sanity
on the table then,

chocolate rabbits
wrapped in brightly inked foils,

their dark heads soon to be bitten off
and eaten,

the foil rolled into tiny balls,
flicked away—

but why should happiness be more transient
than treachery

of all things?—
it seemed like an initiation—

so backstage of the catwalk the tallest woman
slipped out of her cat clothes,

and at the muffler shop
the crawl line reminded viewers repeatedly

that the dead researchers had taken as their clan tag
the name True China Gamers,

and then there were jests
and serious sad agreements to kill for love

inside the dimly-lit school hall then
the 6th graders dashed in & out of *Twelfth Night*

swapping bodies & bespoke clothes—
to the lady Olivia everyone else looked naked

snake-bitten, cross-gartered, or canny,
the thoughts of so many parents in the audience

flew up toward the stage
and inside the pressure drop of lightning & gossip

there was much laughter then.

Master of The Offer

I you me he she it we they—what's
it all about, Dave? For years you don't
make time for cults, don't run toward theories
like a thorny sleepwalker—you putz around, sure,
but as a currency counterfeiter would, with sunglasses
pushed back atop a bald head while checking out
the product—then one day instructed by songs
sung five centuries ago in northern forests
you wake abruptly out of a long summer nap
with late afternoon traffic crawling across
the pea-green Penobscot bridge 100 miles away
from your blinking eyelids, & it comes to you,
the details, the specifications, the whole story,
like an accidental leak of private credit data
it comes to remind you that everyone is on record
and accounted for, & everyone admits it sooner or later,
accepts or refuses, is the Master of The Offer, learns
after moseying about to put up or shut up. Time
to give up what's left of arrested development.
Time to cancel your appointment with faithlessness.

Camus

Suppose on the water of this river
it were written-out

in scribbles like
so, put down to tell us

(as if we needed the demandingly
loyal Camus to tell us)

that "we suffocate among people who
think they are always right,

absolutely right, whether
in their machines

or in their ideas"—suppose
it were written there

at the river's widest bend,
in accord with the law

of karmic translation
and proven

hydrography—
would it stop you? Would you

love any less the sounds
of a Sunday afternoon? the river

with its rowers pony-dogging
downstream, & the oar

splash of a single scull
winking back as

sunlight sugar-mapled
in the water flow—the fact of endless

murder far off, death
in the name of abstractions,

the echoes of pitiless thoughts
hammered-out in the air

of a mosque or a lecture hall
at the Naval War College, windowless,

full of thunderbolts & buzz cuts
and talk of targeting platforms,

all of it far away—"we kill, & are killed,
by proxy"—is this a problem?

(should it be?), this pleasure,
or that you

smiled last night
as you eavesdropped

upon an intuitive cat
after it had wandered up to a priest

unbidden, the cobblestones wet
with an amiable rain. If

you were alive all
these years, what would you say

happened? a black & white cat
performed a Petipa

adagio? or else
in the mother-of-pearl heat haze

someone's back was bent,
an oar stroked?—that simple?

Whose Country, Mine or Theirs?

It's a problem as small
as a birch leaf blown against a window screen—
this clinging bit of green
inside of which at the end of day
you can see a forest crossroad & a dim figure halfway
between a so-called Zion & a wired so-called Babylon,
tho whether he is being carried away or is returning from captivity
that is unclear
in those smoking piney-woods
he appears to be
waiting to be fed—
after which the leaf will fall.

Lightning with Stag in Its Glare

There was a hollow dry gourd hot with energies,
and inside was the thunder of Chinese healing herbs,
and the powers of inexplicable oils & unguents, & pouches
full of insect wings. Later there was the kind of storm
that kills, a real storm, the kind that knows an oak is strong.
There was lightning with a stag in its glare then. And
microorganisms. At the lake, on a canvas beach chair,
someone lovely & stubborn had left a red & yellow plum.
There was a woodpecker too, perhaps a half mile away
in a boisterous elm. And ahead of us, on a sandy hillside,
the Jet Propulsion Lab; the elegant equations there that worked
inside of women & men & machines. And beyond all of this
was compassion. Or the complicities of the wicked. Covenants
to transfer power. Demands for obedience. Great charity. Dread.
Some mornings began with a well-ironed handkerchief,
a *whiskey blanc* or cantaloupe. Others started with a maple—
the flirtatious, green-eyed maple that overnight had sprouted
full-blown from the cellar of a power plant burned-down years ago.
The mornings were so flavorful, so unintentional. Mostly
there was cruelty, courtesy, murder & randy love stares.
With or without runway lighting or makeup
the starvelings of fashion walked swiftly among us
looking new in the sunlight's sweep. They were unrecognizable.
Indentured. Redeemed. We were all unrecognized.
All of us were unsure if our names were our true names
or slave names. And soon enough there was rain
over all the Elizabeths. And a skiff embarked across the bay.
But no student at exam time in any school anywhere
would claim this has a storyline or plot. Only now & again
did it make sense. It was when one of us took a turn
as the bird—that woodpecker in the elm—out of the tree
the bird would fly & for ten or fifteen minutes then the rest

of us could hear it tapping its beak against an old church bell—
as if this was what we were born for—a lifetime that passed
in just ten or fifteen minutes while you tried hard to drill
through an alloy of brain-forged copper & iron and it rang.

Acknowledgments

Some of these poems first appeared, often in different versions, in the following magazines, to whose editors a grateful acknowledgement is made:

The Alaska Quarterly Review: "Birthday" and "Pasted Up in the Vicinity of the Sun"

The American Poetry Review: "To Answer," "Camus," "Forehead," "Hidden," "How Else to Say It," "Lightning with Stag in Its Glare," "All the Way from Murasakino," "Nostalgia," "Otherwise Elsewhere," "Powers," "The Same Bourgeois Magic Wherever the Mailtrain Sets You Down," "To Lynda Hull," "Wandering Oxygen," "Whose Country, Mine or Theirs?" and "Wishes"

Cave Wall: "Lay It Down"

New Ohio Review: "Outbound Fall River 1967" and "Wordsworthian"

Pilot: "Slightly More Alone" and "Something That You'll Never Know Can Hurt the Quiet of a Sunday Morning"

Ploughshares: "Double Elegy, with Curse" and "Somewhere between a Row of Traffic Cones and the Country Once Called Burma"

Prairie Schooner: "Achievement" and "Pirated Music"

Smartish Pace: "Crush"

Tuesday: "The Question inside Tuesday"

Tufts Magazine: "To Simone"

Thanks most to my family and friends, as ever.

David Rivard is the author of four previous books of poetry: *Sugartown, Bewitched Playground, Wise Poison,* and *Torque.* He has received the James Laughlin Award of the Academy of American Poets, the Agnes Lynch Starrett Poetry Prize, and the O. B. Hardison, Jr. Poetry Prize from the Folger Shakespeare Library, as well as grants from the Guggenheim Foundation, the National Endowment for the Arts, and the Howard Foundation. He teaches in the graduate writing program at the University of New Hampshire and lives in Cambridge, Massachusetts.

Book composition by
BookMobile Design and Publishing Services, Minneapolis, Minnesota.
Manufactured by Versa Press on acid-free paper.